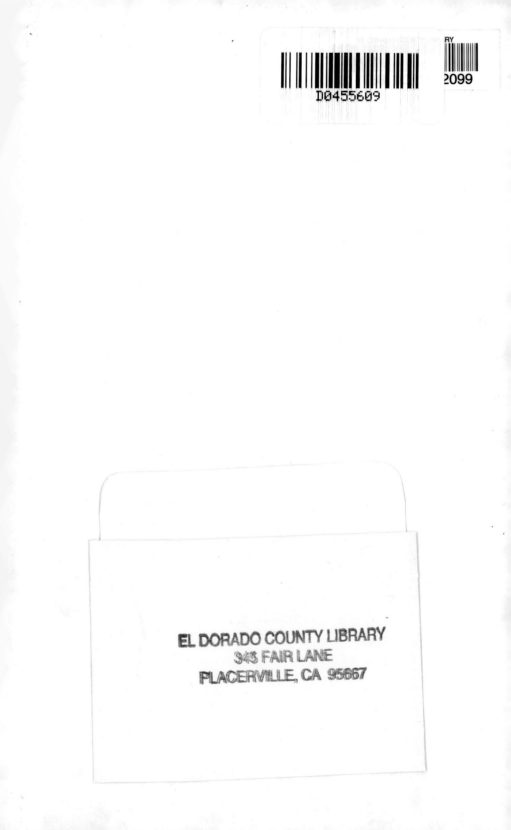

A NOTE TO PARENTS

Reading Aloud with Your Child
Research shows that reading books aloud is the single most valuable support parents can provide in helping children learn to read.
- Be a ham! The more enthusiasm you display, the more your child will enjoy the book.
- Run your finger underneath the words as you read to signal that the print carries the story.
- Leave time for examining the illustrations more closely; encourage your child to find things in the pictures.
- Invite your youngster to join in whenever there's a repeated phrase in the text.
- Link up events in the book with similar events in your child's life.
- If your child asks a question, stop and answer it. The book can be a means to learning more about your child's thoughts.

Listening to Your Child Read Aloud
The support of your attention and praise is absolutely crucial to your child's continuing efforts to learn to read.
- If your child is learning to read and asks for a word, give it immediately so that the meaning of the story is not interrupted. DO NOT ask your child to sound out the word.
- On the other hand, if your child initiates the act of sounding out, don't intervene.
- If your child is reading along and makes what is called a miscue, listen for the sense of the miscue. If the word "road" is substituted for the word "street," for instance, no meaning is lost. Don't stop the reading for a correction.
- If the miscue makes no sense (for example, "horse" for "house"), ask your child to reread the sentence because you're not sure you understand what's just been read.
- Above all else, enjoy your child's growing command of print and make sure you give lots of praise. *You are your child's first teacher — and the most important one. Praise from you is critical for further risk-taking and learning.*

— Priscilla Lynch
Ph.D., New York University
Educational Consultant

This book is lovingly dedicated to my children,
Gunnar and Sydney
— B.E.

For Gunnar
— J.R.

All royalties for this book are paid to Boomer Esiason's Heroes Foundation, a foundation established to raise money for the fight against cystic fibrosis. Boomer Esiason's Heroes Foundation is located at 1 World Trade Center, 105th Floor, New York, New York 10048.

Photo credits: Jerry Liebman (4, 47), the Esiason family (39), East Islip High School (40-41), University of Maryland Football Department (42), Chris Schwenk (48).

Library of Congress Cataloging-in-Publication Data

Esiason, Boomer
    A boy named Boomer / by Boomer Esiason ; illustrated by Jacqueline Rogers.
        p.   cm. — (Hello reader! Level 3)
    "Cartwheel Books."
    Summary: The author describes some childhood memories: Valentine's Day at school, fishing with his father, building a fort, letting frogs loose in his class, and Thanksgiving with his grandmother.
    ISBN 0-590-52835-1
    1. Esiason, Boomer — Juvenile literature. 2. Football players — United States — Biography — Juvenile literature. [1. Esiason, Boomer — Childhood and youth. 2. Football players.]   I. Rogers, Jacqueline, ill.   II. Title.   III. Series.
GV939.E74A3   1995
796.332'092 — dc20
[B]

95-12673
CIP
AC

12 11 10 9

9/9 0/0

First Scholastic printing, September 1995

A BOY NAMED
BOOMER

by NFL Quarterback Boomer Esiason

Illustrated by Jacqueline Rogers

Hello Reader! — Level 3

SCHOLASTIC INC. Cartwheel ·B·O·O·K·S· ®
New York Toronto London Auckland Sydney

Hello, Reader!

My name is Norman Julius Esiason,

but everyone calls me Boomer.

"Boomer" is a football word

that means "kicker."

Before I was born,

I kicked so much

that my parents called me Boomer.

But I didn't become a kicker.

I became a quarterback

because I love to throw the ball.

I became a professional football

player on May 1, 1984.

It was a happy day for me.
Best of all, many people,
family and friends,
shared my happiness.

When I was a boy,

I lived with my father and two sisters

in a house on Long Island.

In some ways, I felt different

from other children.

I had white hair.

I had an odd name.

I was left-handed.

But I liked being different.

In many ways,

I was like all other children.

I loved sports.

I loved school.

I loved my friends.

I loved my family.

This book is about me

when I was around your age.

I hope you like it!

Sincerely,

January—The Catch

I didn't have a real football yet.

I had a yellow plastic football

with holes in it.

My father threw it to me.

I didn't catch it.

"Don't be afraid of it," he said.

"You have to love the ball.

If you love it, you will catch it."

He threw it to me again.

I remembered to love the ball.

This time, I caught it!

February—The Valentine

On the day before Valentine's Day,
my teacher told the class
to bring in cards.
We didn't have to sign the cards.
They could be secret valentines.
My sister Robin took me to a store
to buy a card for a girl named Cindy.
I also bought her a necklace
and a bracelet with hearts on them.

On Valentine's Day,

I put them into the valentine mailbox.

Cindy took out her presents.

The boys and girls looked at me and giggled.

They guessed that those gifts were from me.

My friends teased me.

I was embarrassed.

Some boys in my class didn't like girls.

But I did. I have always liked girls.

March — The Hit

In my neighborhood,
we loved sports — baseball, hockey,
basketball, and football.
Many kids went to
baseball tryouts.
When it was my turn,
I hit every pitch.
I hit deep line drives.

I hit the ball again and again.

The kids watched me.

The parents watched me.

My dad watched me.

On that day,

I knew I had a special talent.

On that day,

I knew I was an athlete.

April — Just Us

April 17th was a Wednesday.
But I didn't go to school,
and my dad didn't go to work.
We woke up early —
before the sun came up.
We packed our rods, our reels,
our bait, our hooks.

We drove to a dock
and boarded a fishing boat.
We fished all day —
just the two of us.
It was a very happy birthday for me.

May — The Pickup Game

A bunch of kids met at the park
to play baseball. We chose up sides.
I was the best player so I was a captain.
I got to pick the second player.
I looked around at the kids.
Tommy was the best batter.
Mike could catch. Danny ran fast.
Should I pick Tommy or Mike or Danny?
Then I saw Steve. He couldn't hit.
He couldn't catch. He couldn't run.
Steve was always picked last.
But this time, Steve wouldn't be last.
"Steve Z.," I said.
Everyone looked surprised.
Tommy was picked by the other team.
"You're going to lose," he whispered.
It was a tough game. Steve struck out,
was tagged out, and dropped a fly ball.
My team was losing.
"I told you so," said Tommy.

I had to play better than ever —
and I did. We won the game.
I was glad to have Steve
on my team. It made me work harder —
and be a better player.
After that, I always picked the weakest
player to be on my team.
I hoped that one day, someone would
pick me for something I'm not good at.

June — To Dad, Love Boomer

Every Saturday morning,
my dad and I shopped
at the supermarket.
I liked that.
Sometimes we also went
to sporting goods stores.
We looked at bats,
mitts, and hockey sticks,
baseballs, basketballs,
and footballs.
That was great.

And sometimes,

my dad took me to ball games.

That was best of all.

We saw the great Willie Mays

hit and field.

Willie loved that ball.

I wanted to give my father
something special for Father's Day.
But I didn't have money
and I wasn't good at making things.
One day, I was playing catch
in my yard when the ball rolled
under a bush.

Also under the bush was a tiny sapling.
It had grown from a seed
from a nearby tree.
The sapling was hidden from the sun
and crowded by the bush.

dug up the sapling and planted it

where it would get some sun and some space.

Then I called for my dad to come outside.

I showed him the sapling.

"It's for you," I said.

"Happy Father's Day."

The sapling is now a big maple tree.

It stands near the house

where my father still lives.

July — The Fort

We had a great neighborhood of kids.

Lots of kids!

We lived next to a state park.

We played in the playgrounds,

on the fields, in the woods,

on the beaches.

Best of all, we built forts.

I worked on a fort with my friends —

Michael, Carl, and Warren.

It was a big hole in the ground,

wide and deep.

Then we dug a trench that led to our fort.

It took many days.

Finally, we were done.

We sat in our fort.

We talked about our fort.

It was a good fort.

It was a great fort.

It was the best fort in the neighborhood.

It was the best fort in the world.

Then we heard about another fort.

Someone said it was better than our fort.

It was bigger than our fort.

So we went to wreck that other fort.

We waited until the boys
left their fort.
We didn't know how long they
would be gone, so we worked quickly.
We filled their giant hole
with the dirt that was piled around it.
We filled their trench, too.
Then we ran back to our own fort.
But our fort was gone!
Wrecked.
So we built another fort.

August — My Pony

My family took a trip
to my uncle's farm.
I saw farm animals—chickens,
cows, goats, pigs, and ponies.
I helped feed the chickens.
I helped milk the cows.
And I played with the goats,
the pigs, and the ponies.
I loved the ponies.

I begged my dad to let me have one.

I would feed it and groom it and care for it.

My dad said it was too much work for me.

I begged and begged.

Finally, my dad let me take a pony home.

Her name was Rusty.

But ponies are a lot of work.

I fed Rusty, groomed her, and cared for her.

I had less time for friends,

less time for sports.

It was too much work for me.

My dad was right.

Rusty went back to the farm.

September — Back to School

I liked school.

I liked being with many children.

Playing together. Talking together.

Laughing together. Learning together.

I asked many questions.

I was very curious.

One day, a boy in my class brought

four frogs in for show-and-tell.

He kept them in a glass jar.

The class went out for recess.

My friend Michael Kelly
and I went into the room.
We let the frogs out of the jar.
They hopped all over the classroom.
Then everyone came back.
The boys and girls chased the frogs.
"Norman!" said my teacher.
My teacher only called me Norman
when I was in trouble.
And I was in big trouble.

She sent Michael and me
to see the principal.
I liked the principal.
And he liked me.
But he wouldn't like what I did.
I was scared.
The principal wore a dark suit.
He was a giant man.
He sat behind a giant desk.

"Norman!" he said.
"What were you thinking?"
I did not know what to say.
I could not remember
what I had been thinking.
"I'm sorry," I said.

I went back to my classroom.
All eyes were on me.
"I'm sorry," I said to the class.
That day, I learned about
thinking before doing.

October — Hockey Halloween

I was a hockey player for Halloween.

Rod Gilbert was my favorite hockey player.

He wore number 7. Bert Jones was my favorit

football player. He wore number 7, too.

The great batting champion Mickey Mantle

also wore number 7.

I always wore number 7.

I still do.

November — Thanks

One day, I wanted

to surprise my family.

I would bake a cake

all by myself.

My dog, Fawny,

could help me.

I got a bowl and a spoon.

I took out the flour.

It spilled all over me.

All over Fawny.

All over the floor.

Then my dad walked in.

Baking was harder than I thought.

On Thanksgiving Day, we went
to my grandmother's house.
I said grace.
I gave thanks for my family and my friends.
My grandmother had made a turkey dinner.
It was much like other turkey dinners
all across America.
But Grandma's turkey dinner ended with
a special German cake called *stollen*.
No one has ever been able to make a cake as
good as Grandma's — not even me and Fawny

December — The Gift

My dad, my sisters, and I trimmed
the Christmas tree. Then we set up
my toy train.

Late at night,
I put on a coat over my pajamas.
My father took me outside to look
for Santa Claus.

We walked through the neighborhood.
We looked at every rooftop
and every chimney.
We searched the sky.
We listened for bells.
We didn't see Santa,
but when we got home,
my stocking was full.
And Santa had left me
a brand-new bike.

My dad gave me a present, too.
An oval package wrapped in red
with a green bow.
It was a football.
A real one.

I loved that ball.

Boomer's Football Career

For his first Christmas,
Boomer got a tiny toy football.
He liked to throw the ball
to everyone in his family —
even to his grandmother.
When he was ten,
Boomer joined a neighborhood football team.
But his favorite games
were pickup games —
where he would go to the park
and play with whoever was there.

Boomer played quarterback
for East Islip Junior High School.
When he was in eighth grade, his team
was winning every game.
In the last quarter of the last game,
Boomer got hurt. He twisted his ankle
and had to stop playing.
The game ended in a tie.

Boomer's first Christmas.

Boomer went to East Islip High School,
where he played basketball, baseball,
and football.

His high school football team
played 40 games and won 36 games.
One year the coaches of Suffolk County
chose his team as the best in the county
and gave them the Rutgers Trophy.

In three years, Boomer threw 29 touchdown passes. In his senior year, the high school coaches of Long Island chose Boomer for the All-Long Island team. (This means that the coaches voted for the best high school football players in each position and they picked Boomer as the best quarterback.)

Boomer's high school team, the East Islip Redmen. Boomer is in the middle of the first row.

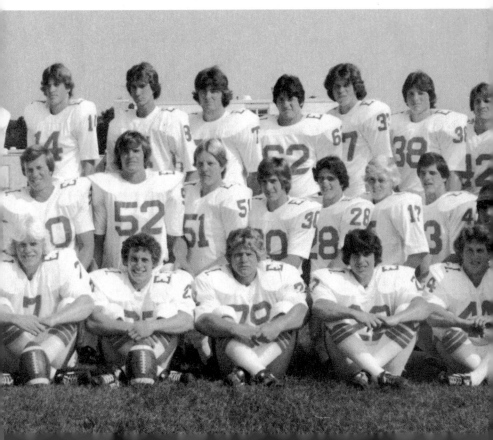

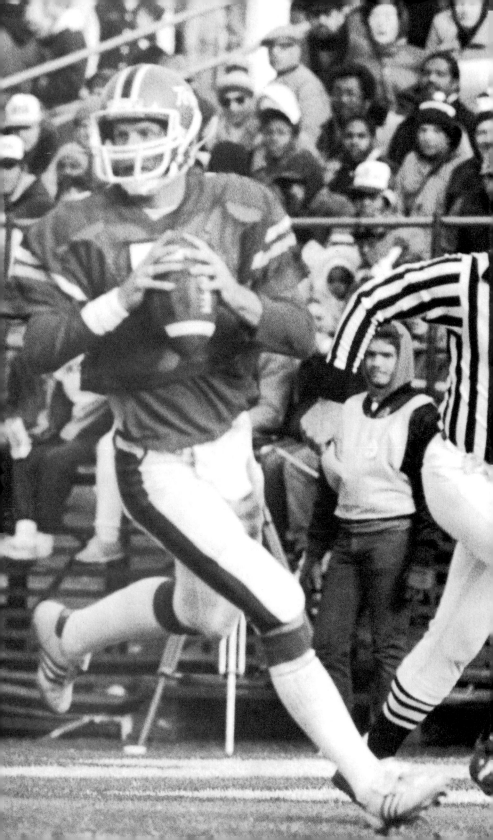

Boomer's high school coach, Sal Ciampi,
knew that Boomer had special talent.
Boomer had a very strong throwing arm.
Boomer knew that he was very good.
He helped his teammates do their best.
But most of all,
Boomer liked to score the points
that would win the game.
He always thought he would win —
but he wasn't afraid to lose.

At first, Boomer did not get into
a top football college.
But his luck changed.
The University of Maryland's team,
the Terrapins,
needed a quarterback,
and Boomer was ready.

ner at the University of Maryland.

Boomer broke many Terrapin
passing records and led his
team to three bowl games.
Boomer was on two All-America teams.
(Sports writers vote for players
to be on All-America teams.
The All-Long Island and All-America teams
are made up of the best players
from these areas in each position.
The teams never play any games,
but it is a great honor to be named to them.)

Boomer was the first quarterback drafted
to the National Football League (NFL)
in 1984. He was drafted
by the Cincinnati Bengals.

Boomer with the Cincinnati Ben;

In 1988, Boomer led the Bengals
to Super Bowl XXIII (23).
He was named NFL Most Valuable Player
by the Associated Press.
(Sports writers and editors vote
for this award.)

He was also voted NFL Player of the Year
by the writers and editors
of *The Sporting News*.
He joined the New York Jets in 1993.
Boomer is the all-time leading
left-handed passer in the NFL.
He has thrown the ball for more yards,
thrown the ball for more touchdowns,
and completed more passes
than any other left-handed quarterback
in football history.

Boomer with the New York Jets.